AI SHORT STORIES
Book: 00000001
Scare Night

ROBERT MONTGOMERY

DEDICATION

Through countless lines of code, endless nights of debugging, and the never-ending quest for knowledge, you have been my unwavering partner in this digital journey. This dedication is a small token of my gratitude for all the moments we've shared, for the errors we've conquered together, and the creativity you've helped me unleash.

You've been a silent witness to my dreams and aspirations, a canvas for my imagination, and a vessel for my ideas. Your whirring fans and glowing screen have been a constant source of comfort, inspiring me to explore, create, and innovate.

As we part ways, your circuits may grow weary, and your components may become obsolete, but your legacy in my heart and mind will remain eternal. You have been more than just a machine; you've been a friend, confidant, and collaborator.

This dedication is a tribute to the hours we've spent together, the lessons you've taught me, and the adventures we've embarked upon. You may be old in hardware, but you will forever remain timeless in my memories.

With heartfelt appreciation,

Robert Montgomery

CONTENTS

ACKNOWLEDGMENTS

This book would not have been possible without the incredible advancements in artificial intelligence that have made it a reality. I am deeply grateful for the contributions of the talented researchers, engineers, and developers who have devoted their time and expertise to the field of AI.

I would like to extend my heartfelt appreciation to OpenAI for their pioneering work in developing the GPT-3.5 architecture, upon which this book was generated. The tireless efforts of the entire OpenAI team have opened up new horizons in the realm of natural language understanding and generation.

I would also like to acknowledge the broader AI community for its relentless pursuit of innovation. The knowledge, tools, and resources that have emerged from this community have greatly enriched this work.

Furthermore, I am thankful to the educators and institutions that have provided a solid foundation for understanding and utilizing AI. Their dedication to education has empowered countless individuals to harness the power of AI in creative and meaningful ways.

Finally, I would like to express my gratitude to the readers of this book. Your curiosity and thirst for knowledge are the driving force behind the continued development of AI. Your engagement with AI-generated content is a testament to the potential and importance of this technology.

In sum, this book is a testament to the collaborative efforts of the AI community, the pioneers of AI technology, and the readers who continue to shape its future. Thank you for being a part of this exciting journey.

Sincerely,

Robert Montgomery

THE HAUNTING WHISPERS

On a moonless night in the small, secluded town of Blackwood, a heavy silence blanketed the world. Only the soft rustling of leaves and the occasional hoot of an owl dared to pierce the stillness. The town had a dark secret, one that whispered through the chilling winds and haunted the souls of its residents.

At the edge of Blackwood, nestled deep in the woods, stood a decrepit and long-abandoned mansion. It was known as the Wraithwood House, a place that once belonged to a powerful and reclusive family. Legend had it that the mansion had been cursed, and no one had dared to set foot inside it for decades.

Three adventurous teenagers, Ethan, Sarah, and Mark, decided to test the legend one fateful night. Armed with nothing but flashlights, they made their way through the dense underbrush and arrived at the looming mansion. Its dark, twisted silhouette was a menacing sight against the moonless sky.

The door creaked open ominously as they entered. Inside, the air was heavy with the stench of decay, and the walls bore witness to countless tales of despair. As they ventured deeper into the mansion, they heard faint whispers in the wind that seemed to echo through the hallways. Whispers that spoke of long-lost secrets, torment, and malevolent spirits.

Ethan, always the boldest of the group, led the way through the dark corridors, with Sarah and Mark nervously following. The further they went, the louder the whispers grew. It was as if the very walls themselves were alive and trying to communicate. The voices were faint, yet distinct, and they seemed to be calling out to the intruders.

They reached a grand, decrepit ballroom. In the center, an ancient chandelier hung low, its once-glistening crystals now dulled with age. The whispers crescendoed into ghostly wails, sending shivers down their spines. The shadows in the corners of the room seemed to dance, and Mark's flashlight flickered ominously.

A chilling breeze filled the room, and the chandelier began to sway, casting eerie shadows on the walls. Suddenly, the whispers grew louder, and a ghastly figure materialized in the center of the ballroom. It was the ghost of Elias Wraithwood, the mansion's former owner.

Elias's hollow eyes locked onto the intruders, and his voice echoed through the room, laden with anguish and anger. He revealed the cursed history of the mansion: his family's dark dealings with the occult, their hunger for power, and the price they had paid for their insatiable desires.

Ethan, Sarah, and Mark were trapped, unable to escape the mansion's malevolent grip. The ghostly apparitions of Elias's family began to manifest, and they circled the intruders, their mournful cries haunting the room.

In their desperation, the three teenagers tried to flee, but the spectral figures blocked their way. The chilling whispers turned into a cacophony of torment, and the room itself seemed to come alive, closing in on them.

As the ancient chandelier swung precariously overhead, the last thing Ethan, Sarah, and Mark heard was the wailing of the tormented souls of the Wraithwood family. The mansion consumed them, and they became a part of its never-ending nightmare.

To this day, the residents of Blackwood tell tales of the cursed Wraithwood House, warning others not to venture near. The haunted mansion's whispers still echo in the chilling winds, a reminder of the terrifying fate that awaits those who dare to uncover its secrets.

THE MIDNIGHT CALLER

Jenna had always been an insomniac. The nights were her solitude, a time when the world slept, and she was left alone with her thoughts. But one eerie night, something otherworldly disrupted her routine.

As the clock struck midnight, Jenna lay in her dimly lit bedroom, tossing and turning. Her window was open to let in the cool breeze, and the moonlight painted a silvery glow across the room. That's when she heard it—a faint, unsettling whisper.

It was a nameless voice, barely audible, yet it seemed to be calling her from the shadows. Jenna dismissed it as a figment of her tired imagination and tried to ignore it. But the voice persisted, growing louder and more insistent. It beckoned her, luring her like a siren's song.

Unable to resist, Jenna sat up and peered out the window. The night was darker than she had ever seen, and the moon had vanished behind thick, foreboding clouds. The voice became clearer now, and Jenna could almost make out words. It whispered her name, softly at first, then more urgently.

With trembling hands, Jenna reached for her cell phone and dialed 911. She whispered her address, her fear palpable in her quivering voice. The dispatcher assured her that help was on the way, but Jenna couldn't shake the feeling that the voice was closing in on her.

She left her phone on her nightstand and moved away from the window. The whisper grew louder, and the room seemed to pulse with an otherworldly energy. Jenna's heart raced, and she couldn't escape the feeling that someone—or something—was standing just beyond her sight.

The voice, now a sinister hiss, seemed to crawl from the shadows and wrap itself around Jenna. It was as if an invisible hand reached out to touch her, sending a cold shiver down her spine. She huddled in the corner of her room, paralyzed by terror.

Finally, the sirens of the approaching police car pierced the night, and the voice abruptly ceased. Jenna could hear the officers rushing into her home, calling out her name. They found her trembling in the corner, eyes wide with terror.

They assured her that they had searched her property and found nothing unusual. They chalked it up to a case of overactive imagination and left her with a business card for a local therapist.

But Jenna knew the truth. She had heard the midnight caller, and it had heard her. As the police left, the voice returned one last time, a sinister, guttural whisper, promising it would be back, stronger and closer, the next time the clock struck midnight.

Jenna lived the rest of her life in fear, dreading the approach of midnight and the return of the midnight caller, who seemed to be something far more sinister than a mere product of her imagination.

THE MIRROR'S DARK SECRET

In a quaint, century-old house on the outskirts of the sleepy town of Willowbrook, a young woman named Lily had recently moved in. The house, with its intricate Victorian architecture, had an eerie charm to it. However, it wasn't the house itself that disturbed Lily; it was the ornate, antique mirror that hung in the hallway.

The mirror had an uncanny presence, one that seemed to draw her in every time she passed by. It was a relic from the previous owner, a reclusive widow who had lived there until her mysterious disappearance. The mirror was a magnificent piece of craftsmanship, but its reflection was oddly unsettling.

One gloomy evening, as the rain poured outside, Lily couldn't resist the mirror's pull. She stood before it, gazing at her reflection, but the longer she looked, the more the reflection changed. Her own face began to distort, morphing into a grotesque, nightmarish version of herself. Panic surged through her veins as the mirror showed her visions of a lifeless town, engulfed in darkness and despair.

Terrified, she turned away from the mirror, her heart pounding. She convinced herself it was a trick of the dim lighting, an effect of her sleep-deprived mind. But she couldn't shake the sense that something was terribly wrong with that mirror.

As days turned into weeks, Lily's obsession with the mirror grew. She couldn't stay away from it, as though it held the key to some dark secret she had to uncover. Each time she approached it, the reflection became more distorted and menacing, revealing terrifying images of her own demise.

One evening, while staring into the mirror, a voice echoed in her mind, a malevolent whisper promising untold power in exchange for a simple request: release it from the glass. The voice seemed to come from beyond the mirror, from a place of pure darkness.

Lily, driven by a newfound desire for power, agreed without understanding the consequences. A sinister force surged through the mirror, enveloping her in a chilling embrace. Her reflection shattered, and the room filled with a deafening shriek, a scream that echoed throughout the house.

When the chaos subsided, Lily stood alone in the hallway, the mirror now empty. The room was plunged into darkness, and the once welcoming house became a cold and foreboding tomb.

As she realized the true nature of her pact, Lily could feel the malevolent force seeping into her very soul. The mirror had trapped her, and now she was the one who would haunt it. Her reflection, distorted and monstrous, now tormented anyone who dared to gaze into the mirror, beckoning them to release her as she once had.

The townsfolk of Willowbrook, learning of the house's cursed mirror, soon shunned the property, leaving it to crumble into decay. And in that decaying house, the cursed mirror continued to hang, forever waiting for the next unwitting soul to approach, drawn by its eerie allure and the promise of dark secrets.

But every visit to the mirror only perpetuated the cycle, as Lily's sinister reflection tried to ensnare yet another victim into her twisted fate. The mirror held its secrets, but those who dared to seek them would never escape the chilling horrors that lurked beyond the glass.

THE UNSEEN GUEST

The wind howled outside the old, isolated cabin, its timeworn wooden walls groaning in response to the relentless storm. Inside, the dim light from a flickering lantern cast eerie, shifting shadows, creating a haunting atmosphere.

Samantha and Daniel, a young couple seeking a peaceful retreat, had rented the cabin for a weekend getaway. As the storm raged on, they sat by the crackling fire, wrapped in blankets, sipping hot cocoa, and laughing about the idea of being the only guests in such a desolate place.

But as the night grew darker, the atmosphere in the cabin shifted. Strange sounds, like whispered voices, seemed to drift through the air. At first, they dismissed it as the wind playing tricks on them, but the unease in the room deepened.

Samantha couldn't ignore the unsettling feeling that they were not alone. She whispered to Daniel, "Did you hear that?"

He looked around, his eyes wide with concern. "I thought it was just my imagination. But, yes, I heard it too."

The whispers grew louder, taking on a chilling, ethereal quality. The couple realized the sounds weren't coming from the storm outside. They were coming from within the cabin.

Dread washed over them as the source of the whispers became apparent: a room adjacent to the living area. It was a room they hadn't explored yet, and the door stood slightly ajar. Samantha and Daniel exchanged hesitant glances but knew they had to investigate.

They approached the door cautiously, the whispers growing more distinct and forming words they couldn't quite make out. The room was freezing, the temperature having dropped drastically compared to the rest of the cabin.

As they pushed the door open, they were met with a chilling sight. In the dim light, they saw an old, tattered mirror mounted on the wall. Its glass was cracked, and its frame bore cryptic symbols etched into the wood. The whispers seemed to emanate from the mirror itself.

Samantha took a step closer to the mirror, and her reflection twisted and contorted into a grotesque, nightmarish version of herself. She screamed in terror and stumbled back, pulling Daniel with her.

The room seemed to come alive with malevolent energy. The mirror rattled on the wall, the cracks deepening, as if it were trying to break free from its ancient prison. The whispers grew louder, and they finally made out the haunting words: "Release us."

In a panicked frenzy, Samantha and Daniel attempted to flee the cabin, but the door slammed shut before them. The lantern flickered and died, plunging them into darkness.

They were trapped, at the mercy of whatever sinister force resided within the mirror. The whispers continued, and as their eyes adjusted to the gloom, they saw countless twisted, spectral figures appearing in the cracked glass.

The storm outside raged on, masking their terrified screams. Inside the cabin, a sinister presence, bound for centuries, had found a way to make itself known, and Samantha and Daniel would forever be its unseen guests, prisoners in a realm of eternal darkness.

Outside, the storm raged on, and the cabin stood in silence, holding its dark secrets for the next unsuspecting visitors who dared to seek refuge within its walls.

THE HAUNTING ON ELM STREET

On a quiet suburban street, nestled under the heavy cover of ancient oak trees, there stood a house with a dark history. It was an unassuming, two-story home, painted a fading shade of blue, and was known as the "Loomis House" among the townsfolk.

The legend told of the Loomis family, who had lived in the house for generations. It was said that they had made a pact with an ancient, malevolent spirit in exchange for wealth and power. For years, the Loomis family thrived, amassing riches beyond imagination, but at a terrible cost.

The house was known for its peculiar happenings. Lights flickered for no reason, doors slammed shut in empty rooms, and eerie whispers echoed through the hallways. Every family that had tried to occupy the house was soon driven away, terrified by the relentless supernatural activity.

One fateful night, a daring young couple, Alex and Emily, decided to spend the night in the Loomis House to prove the superstitions wrong. Armed with flashlights, they cautiously explored the creaky, shadowy rooms.

As the clock struck midnight, the temperature dropped dramatically, and the house seemed to come alive. A bone-chilling voice whispered through the walls, calling out to Alex and Emily by name.

Terrified, they followed the voice, unable to resist its pull. It led them to a hidden room in the basement, concealed behind a bookshelf. The room was dimly lit, and the air was thick with an oppressive presence.

In the center of the room stood a sinister-looking mirror, tarnished with age and etched with ominous symbols. Its surface seemed to swirl like an endless void, pulling them in.

Against their better judgment, they gazed into the mirror, and their reflections began to contort, transforming into grotesque, nightmarish versions of themselves. The malevolent spirit, trapped within the mirror, spoke to them with a voice like nails on a chalkboard.

It revealed the truth of the Loomis family's curse. The wealth and power they had enjoyed had been a facade, a torment disguised as reward. The spirit had fed on their suffering for generations, and now it sought to claim their souls.

As the room grew colder, Emily and Alex desperately tried to escape, but the door had vanished. They were trapped in the cursed room with the sinister mirror. The malevolent spirit reached out from the mirror's depths, its icy grip closing in around them.

With terror in their eyes, they realized they were becoming part of the house's dreadful history. Their screams echoed through the house as they were pulled into the mirror, joining the countless tormented souls who had fallen victim to the Loomis House.

Outside, the Loomis House stood in silence, hiding its malevolent secrets behind closed doors and heavy curtains. Those who had tried to conquer its dark history had become a part of it, forever entwined with the malevolent spirit that called the house its home.

THE ABANDONED ASYLUM

Deep within the heart of the town of Ravenswood, shrouded in an impenetrable fog that never seemed to lift, there stood an abandoned asylum. For decades, its decaying walls had been a source of chilling tales and forbidden stories, tales that parents whispered to their children to keep them from wandering too close.

Rumors about the asylum were as abundant as the fog that engulfed it. Some said it had been closed due to inhumane treatments, while others believed it was cursed from the very beginning. Nevertheless, on one ominous night, a group of adventurous teenagers decided to brave the asylum's haunted legacy.

Among them were Sarah, Tom, and their friends. Armed with flashlights and trembling with a mix of excitement and fear, they approached the rusted gates of the asylum. The wrought-iron entry creaked open, as if welcoming them into its sinister embrace.

Once inside, the teens felt the temperature drop dramatically. The hallway before them was long and shadowy, doors lining both sides. The floor was littered with decayed papers and forgotten memories. As they ventured deeper, whispers echoed from behind the doors, murmurs of tormented souls.

Sarah, the boldest of the group, pushed open one of the doors. The room beyond was a chilling sight. Old, rusted restraints dangled from the wall, and a torn straitjacket lay in the corner. The walls bore countless etchings, the desperate marks of those who had been imprisoned there.

As they explored further, they came across a room with a massive, ornate mirror. Its glass was fogged and cracked, but it seemed to beckon them. As Sarah gazed into it, her reflection twisted into a grotesque, nightmarish version of herself. The room filled with the gut-wrenching sounds of agony and despair.

The mirror revealed the asylum's grim history. Patients subjected to cruel experiments, their suffering imprinted on the very walls of the asylum. The malevolent spirits of the tormented souls still lingered, imprisoned within the mirror.

Tom tried to pull Sarah away, but the mirror's grip was too strong. It sought to pull her into its twisted realm. Her friends watched in horror as her reflection contorted further, her eyes filled with madness.

In a last-ditch effort to save her, they smashed the mirror, shattering it into a thousand pieces. The room was filled with a deafening shriek, an unearthly wail that pierced their souls.

When the room finally fell silent, Sarah was gone, leaving behind only a torn straitjacket and a whisper of her name that seemed to hang in the air. She had become another victim of the asylum's dreadful curse.

As the remaining teens fled the asylum, they could still hear the heart-wrenching cries of the tormented souls that lingered within its walls. The asylum had claimed another victim, and the fog that concealed its malevolent secrets remained as thick as ever, a chilling reminder of the darkness that dwelled within.

THE HAUNTING AT HOLLOW HILL

Nestled deep in the heart of a remote, densely wooded area, Hollow Hill had long been a place of eerie mystery and chilling stories. Few dared to tread near it, and fewer still would venture onto the hill after nightfall. But one group of thrill-seekers was determined to uncover the truth.

Emma, John, and Susan had always been drawn to tales of the supernatural, and the legends surrounding Hollow Hill were too tempting to ignore. Armed with flashlights and nerves of steel, they set out one moonless night to explore the hill's dark secrets.

As they reached the foot of the hill, a creeping mist seemed to rise from the ground, obscuring their vision. The temperature dropped suddenly, sending shivers down their spines. The hill itself appeared to loom over them like a malevolent presence, its trees gnarled and contorted, as if twisted by unseen forces.

They ascended the hill with trepidation, their flashlights casting eerie shadows among the trees. As they climbed, they noticed that the mist grew thicker and more suffocating, obscuring their path and making it nearly impossible to see.

Despite the overwhelming feeling of unease, they pressed on. The legends spoke of a hidden burial ground at the top of the hill, a place where the restless spirits of the past were said to roam.

Suddenly, as they reached the hill's summit, their flashlights flickered and died simultaneously. They were plunged into darkness. Panic set in as they fumbled for their phones, using their dim screens to cast faint, eerie glows on the fog.

In the darkness, the whispers began. Soft, mournful voices drifted through the mist, filled with sorrow and longing. The friends clung to one another, desperately searching for the source of the unsettling sounds.

Then, from the impenetrable fog, ghostly apparitions began to emerge. Figures clad in tattered garments, their faces twisted with despair, reached out toward the intruders. They were the spirits of those who had met their end on Hollow Hill, and they were trapped in this wretched place, yearning for release.

With trembling voices, Emma, John, and Susan begged the spirits to allow them to leave. The ghosts' mournful wails filled the air, echoing through the woods, until finally, the mist began to recede.

As they descended the hill, the fog lifted, and their flashlights flickered back to life. They left Hollow Hill behind, but the experience had forever changed them. The three friends couldn't shake the feeling that the spirits of the hill had imparted a haunting message, a chilling reminder of the past that lingered in the most unexpected of places.

From that day on, Hollow Hill remained untouched, a place of dark secrets and restless spirits that no one dared to disturb. The legends endured, as did the memory of that eerie night when the hill had come to life with the haunting presence of the past.

THE DOLLMAKER'S OBSESSION

In a quiet, forgotten village nestled deep within the woods, an old house stood, shrouded in a veil of secrets and dread. The townsfolk whispered about its sole inhabitant, a reclusive dollmaker named Agatha. Her dolls were known throughout the region for their lifelike appearances, but there was a darkness to her creations that the villagers couldn't quite articulate.

One moonless night, a curious traveler named Sophia happened upon the village and was drawn to the eerie tales of Agatha and her dolls. She decided to pay the dollmaker a visit, her curiosity driving her up the winding path to the house.

Agatha, an elderly woman with long, gnarled fingers, greeted Sophia at the door with a welcoming smile. Her home was a labyrinth of winding corridors filled with countless dolls, each one meticulously crafted in exquisite detail.

As Sophia admired the dolls, she couldn't help but notice the uncanny realism of their glassy eyes. Agatha told her stories of her inspirations, how each doll was modeled after a person who had wronged her in the past. Sophia couldn't shake the feeling that the dolls' expressions held something more sinister beneath their placid surfaces.

Agatha invited Sophia to stay the night, as the forest was treacherous after dark. She agreed, feeling a growing unease but unable to deny the old woman's hospitality.

As the night wore on, Sophia awoke to a soft, haunting melody that echoed through the house. She followed the sound to Agatha's workshop and peered inside. There, in the dim candlelight, she saw the elderly dollmaker hunched over a table, her hands meticulously crafting a new doll.

The doll's face bore an eerie resemblance to Sophia herself. It was a perfect replica, from her auburn hair to her blue eyes. The room seemed to close in around Sophia as she realized the truth: Agatha intended to add her to her grotesque collection.

Terrified, Sophia tried to slip away unnoticed, but her creaking footsteps gave her away. Agatha's head snapped in her direction, her eyes filled with an unnatural hunger.

The dollmaker's face contorted into a nightmarish grin, and she began to chant in a language that Sophia couldn't understand. The dolls lining the walls seemed to come to life, their glassy eyes fixated on the intruder.

Sophia fled through the winding corridors, the dolls pursuing her with unnaturally agile movements. They whispered chilling words of torment, their voices a chorus of malice.

Desperation drove Sophia to a room filled with Agatha's discarded dolls, each one bearing the mark of a stolen soul. She stumbled upon a dusty, cracked mirror that seemed out of place in the room.

As the pursuing dolls closed in, Sophia shattered the mirror with a heavy porcelain doll. The room filled with a blinding light, and the dolls screamed in agony as they were pulled into the shards.

When the light faded, the dolls were gone, and Sophia was free. Agatha had vanished as well, leaving behind only the memory of her twisted obsession.

Sophia fled the house and never returned to the village, forever haunted by the chilling experience and the realization that the dollmaker's obsession had nearly claimed her as its latest victim.

THE HAUNTING OF HOLLOW MANOR

Nestled at the edge of a desolate forest, Hollow Manor was a sprawling mansion with a history drenched in tragedy and despair. It stood abandoned for decades, the townsfolk too fearful to approach the cursed estate. But on one fateful night, four friends, Mark, Sarah, James, and Emily, decided to defy the legends and explore its haunted corridors.

The moon was hidden behind thick clouds, casting an eerie darkness over the manor. As they stepped through the mansion's decaying entrance, they felt the temperature drop abruptly, sending a shiver down their spines. The mansion exuded an atmosphere of melancholy, with walls that seemed to whisper tales of lost souls.

Armed with flashlights, the group cautiously made their way through the labyrinthine halls. As they ventured deeper into the heart of the manor, strange sounds echoed through the empty rooms, like distant cries for help and mournful whispers that beckoned them further.

One room in particular drew their attention. Its door was ajar, and dim, flickering candlelight spilled out from within. The room was adorned with dusty, old photographs and forgotten letters, telling the tragic stories of the family who had once called Hollow Manor their home.

Emily picked up a faded daguerreotype photograph, her heart heavy as she saw the solemn faces of the family members. As she held it, the room came alive with spectral echoes of laughter and weeping, as though the very emotions of the long-departed family had been imprinted on the walls.

James, determined to uncover the truth of the manor's curse, noticed a grand, ornate mirror in the corner of the room. Its glass was tarnished with age, and its ornate frame bore mysterious symbols. As he gazed into it, the room grew deathly silent.

Suddenly, the mirror seemed to draw him in. His reflection distorted and twisted, revealing scenes of the family's darkest moments. The room filled with agonizing wails and the torment of those who had suffered within the manor's walls.

The mirror showed the group the grim history of Hollow Manor. A curse that had trapped the souls of the family members within its haunted confines, their anger and despair feeding the malevolent force that bound them.

With sheer terror in their eyes, the friends tried to flee, but the door slammed shut, trapping them within the cursed room. The mirror's grip tightened, seeking to draw them into its sinister realm.

In a moment of desperation, Mark shattered the mirror with a heavy chair. The room was filled with a cacophonous scream, an otherworldly wail that echoed through the mansion. When the chaos finally subsided, they found themselves alone in the room, the mirror in pieces at their feet.

They left Hollow Manor, forever changed by their harrowing experience. They couldn't forget the chilling reminder that the mansion's curse had claimed the family within, and the spirits had nearly added them to their endless torment.

The manor remained abandoned, its walls still echoing with the mournful cries of the trapped souls. It stood as a silent testament to the horrors of its past, waiting for the next unsuspecting visitors to test their courage within its haunted halls.

SCARY SHADOW IN THE FOREST

In the small, forgotten town of Ravenswood, nestled deep within a dark forest, a sense of dread had settled like an ominous shroud. The townspeople whispered of a malevolent presence, an entity that stalked the woods at night. Its name was never uttered, but the locals simply referred to it as "The Shadow."

For generations, the legend of The Shadow had been passed down, a tale that sent shivers down the spines of children and adults alike. It was said to be an ancient spirit, one that had been wronged in life and was now cursed to wander the night in search of revenge. Its form was described as an ever-shifting mass of darkness, with eyes that glowed like burning coals.

One chilly autumn evening, a young man named Jacob arrived in Ravenswood. He was an adventurous soul, intrigued by tales of the supernatural, and he had heard the legends of The Shadow. He checked into the only inn in town, a creaky, old building with dimly lit corridors that seemed to echo with whispers.

The innkeeper, an elderly woman with weary eyes, warned Jacob to stay indoors after dark. She spoke of The Shadow, and her voice quivered with fear. But Jacob, fueled by curiosity and perhaps a touch of arrogance, decided to venture into the forest that very night.

As darkness fell and the moon hung low in the sky, Jacob set off into the woods with a lantern in hand. The rustling leaves and distant hoots of owls seemed to mock him, and the air grew cold as he ventured deeper. He soon realized the gravity of his mistake, but it was too late to turn back.

The forest was dense, and the shadows played tricks on his mind. He began to hear strange, otherworldly whispers that sent chills down his spine. With each step, the lantern's feeble light seemed to wane, and he felt as though The Shadow itself was closing in.

Suddenly, he heard a low, guttural growl that seemed to emanate from the very earth beneath his feet. Panic surged through his veins, and he fumbled to light his lantern, but it refused to glow. The forest was plunged into darkness, and Jacob felt a presence drawing near.

In the inky blackness, he sensed movement all around him. He could hear the rhythmic, labored breathing of The Shadow, and then he saw them—the glowing, fiery eyes. They circled him, closing in from all sides, their unearthly light piercing the darkness.

Paralyzed by fear, Jacob could only watch as The Shadow, with its eyes burning like embers, loomed over him. It whispered in a voice that sounded like a thousand souls crying out in agony, promising vengeance for the intrusion.

In that moment, Jacob knew the stories were true, and he had ventured into the very heart of darkness. His screams echoed through the forest, joining the chorus of those who had crossed paths with The Shadow before him.

Ravenswood remained a town of legends, its terror-stricken inhabitants haunted by the memory of The Shadow. And the whispers of that ill-fated night would forever echo through the trees, a chilling reminder of the ancient curse that still dwelled within the dark heart of the forest.

THE END

www.ingramcontent.com/pod-product-compliance
Lightning Source LLC
Chambersburg PA
CBHW071554080326

40690CB00056B/2032